Crococ

A play by Samantha Grierson

To Little Green and my 3 Monkeys
with all of my love

Reviews

"It made me feel emotional and it made me laugh"

Russ Litten, author of Scream If You Want To Go Faster, Swear Down and Kingdom

"This is amazing! Crocodile's voice works so well"

Tiffany Murray author of Diamond Star Halo, Ghost Moth and Happy Accident

Crocodile

Crocodile 8 and Crocodile 32 played by same actor

Beau

Pete – non speaking part

Syd

No extras. The play takes place over a few days in London, with flashbacks to Yorkshire in the mid-1990s. This is achieved with overhead screen as a video.

Overview

Crocodile is fast talking, fast acting and does whatever occurs to her. Her best mate Beau tries to keep her on track and her irreverent sense of humour goes someway to curb her behaviour…. enter Syd… a decorator with a love of ice cream and looking for something more…. exit Crocodile who is always looking for something different, until she isn't.

 A bitter sweet play that navigates identity, neurodiversity, loss, love and mushrooms.

Written by Samantha Grierson

www.crabandbull.com First Edition

Act I
Scene 1

Interior Day. Inside a small flat in London. Chaotic, items piled everywhere. Crocodile is crashing around. Crocodile is random, chaotic and does whatever occurs to her. She is fluid in every way and has no defined boundaries, despite following lots of inbuilt rules. She is making a bagel out of a piece of toast with a blow torch, goggles on, bandana on.

Voice over, Crocodile, (*accent soft Yorkshire*)

My name is Crocodile Armitage. Most people call me Croc. I probably have some other name on a birth certificate somewhere, but no one could remember such a detail. I was born on the floor of a Post Office, as that was where she went into labour with me. As the contractions started. She just sat down and waited and waited and finally pushed. I grew up in a shipwrecked cottage on the edge of a village in Yorkshire, with Vandaline. (*Pause*)

I'm 32 now and live in London in this flat above a Buddhist shop and a Chinese takeaway. I'm making a bagel. I have run out of bagels. I like bagels. It's gluten free. I like tomato paste too because it tastes like fascination. I only have two emotions, bored and curious. Apparently bored and curious are not emotions, so maybe I don't have any. But curious should be an emotion, because that's how I feel most of the time. I just wonder what will happen. In fact, I don't just wonder, I do. If I have a good idea, I see it through and see where it takes me. It doesn't always end well. I'm trying to teach myself, self-control and just sit with things for a while and not act. So, I've written down all of the ideas that I have had today, that I didn't do and tore it all up and then it occurred to me to burn them.

Crocodile lifts up a pot with torn up paper inside of it. She opens the window and puts it on the windowsill. She takes the blow torch. It burns gently at first and then bursts into a whoosh of flames. She reacts and pours a bottle of coke over the cooking pot. She lifts the papers out. The papers didn't burn.

Act I
Scene 2

Interior day. Office in London somewhere, tower block setting. Crocodile is sitting opposite a work colleague, Beau, she is 30 and of African origin. She speaks in long sentences without breathing. Crocodile is wearing a male tailored suit with a pink sun top underneath and random jewelry.

Crocodile

What am I supposed to do with this? (*Pointing at her laptop screen*)

Beau

With what? Would you like to shed a little further light on the question, rather than just stating – this? I may need more of a frame of reference because god knows what you have got up on your screen. How to grow artichokes in recycled demijohns?

Crocodile

With this 3 page email from Git boy. I can't read it. It's like pain.

Beau

10:12 Re: Product development and profit targets? From our most esteemed lord and master who is seeking his next promotion as we speak?

Crocodile

Yup that one. Have you read it? I refuse.

Beau

Yeah, I'm on the final recommendations and speculative conclusions, aka telling him what he wants to hear. We have to have our papers in by 5, haven't you started yet?

Crocodile

I don't read emails that are longer than 3 lines. Have you met me? Nothing good that needs to be said goes beyond 3 lines, it's like a law of nature. Can you give me the bullet points? This job is the worst job that I have ever had ever, in the history of ever. I'm going to look for a new one. (*She stands up and starts to pace, playing with her mobile*).

Beau

The bullet points of a project brief that needs writing by the end of the day that you haven't even started yet? (*Pause*) Stop looking for new jobs.

Crocodile

I wouldn't say that I hadn't started it yet. (*Pause*) I've found one, near Euston (*Pause*). Sent my CV over.

Beau

How can you have started writing something that you haven't even read about to know what to start yet?

Crocodile

Because I always have ideas waiting to be written down, I just need to know which one of my ideas he wants writing about this time (*Sits down again*). It says you can work from home.

Beau

He wants a 5 page approach on profit margin improvement for non-watch based time instruments.

Crocodile

Oh that old shit. I can tell him that in 5 words. 'Barking up the wrong tree' *Swings around in chair, bangs her knee with a thump on the desk and knocks both coffee cups over, spilling coffee everywhere. They both swear and clean the desk up.*

Beau

Can you be trusted with anything? Like anything at all that may come to mind to me at any given minute?

Crocodile

I put my website live last night, does that count?

Beau

The website where you are looking for people who have ancestors that lived in large white rural houses in the 1800s in a small region of Lancashire because you are writing a novel set then and don't know what furniture looked like and you thought they might be able to help?

Crocodile

Well the book I bought on eBay didn't help.

Beau

The book that is now out of print so you bought a second-hand copy for £150 just so that you could see a photo of what types of chair people sat in back then? Because you can't imagine it.

Crocodile

It wasn't £150, it was £147. I can't help it if I have no imagination for things I haven't seen. I'm still on the first chapter, I managed to describe the house exterior because I've seen a photo and then I just kind of went dead.

Beau

Do you think writing a historical novel, in a place you have never visited, when you can't even picture a chair back then, in order to finish the first chapter, might be a problem?

Crocodile

Emily Bronte did it.

Beau

Emily fucking Bronte lived then you dip shit, she didn't need to buy a book to know what to sit on!

They work quietly for a minute. Crocodile writes on small bits of paper exuberantly and puts them in a pile next to her, with the others.

Crocodile

I want to grow mushrooms

Beau

Of course you do. Why mushrooms?

Crocodile

Because you can grow them in the dark, you just need mud and the spore things and it's sustainable and it would be good to say that I grow mushrooms for a living, rather than being a corporate drone.

Beau

So mushrooms, and where in your one bedroom flat are you going to grow all of these £100k a year salary providing mushrooms?

Crocodile

In a warehouse. Any warehouse. I don't think mushrooms care. Just get an out of town warehouse, 30,000 square meters or so. Won't cost too much on an industrial estate, it's not like its retail.

Beau

Don't you think you might get a bit sad working in a dark warehouse all day surrounded by mould? You weren't good when we went had that posh work meal in a basement in Shoreditch, you said by the end of the day you were getting Seasonally Adjusted Disorder symptoms.

Crocodile

I was, it was awful. Had to take Vitamin D tablets for 3 months afterwards. Well, I'll be finding that out tomorrow anyway.

Beau

Tomorrow, what's tomorrow?

Crocodile

I'm viewing 3 in Putney

Beau

What?

Crocodile

You think I should view more than 3?

Beau

Woman. I think you should stick to your New Years resolution, the same one you have had for the last 20 years and stop doing every single thing that you think of. I thought you were meant to write them on bits of paper and not do them. When did you have this idea?

Crocodile

This morning, after we discussed Russian train robberies. I am still writing them on bits of paper. I'm just struggling not to act.

Beau

And so you thought, I know I will just go and rent a warehouse and start growing mushrooms in it. Having zero gardening skills or probably knowing any names of any sodding mushroom varieties.

Crocodile

Closed cap. They are the easiest. I've ordered a starter kit from Amazon and I'm doing an online course when I get back later tonight so I will be fine.

Beau

Of course you are. You need to get a handle on this. I understand that it's a coping mechanism for you, all of this... action. (*Pause*). We need to get you a partner... you need to get out more. Have you thought any more about meeting up with my mate Syd? Could be an interesting date?

Crocodile

No. Do they like mushrooms?

Act I
Scene 3

Interior Day. Inside a small ramshackle cottage in Yorkshire, a girls bedroom with a sloping roof that looks like its collapsing. There is a desk made from a cupboard door, propped up on boxes. A few books and random objects. Thin blankets falling off the bed. Then we see the 8 year old Crocodile playing with something on the desk. (Recorded and projected above the stage).

Crocodile aged 8

This is Brave and he's my pet. He's a radish. I've had him now for nearly two years. I keep him in this Tupperware box with a nice bed of pencil sharpenings for warmth. I talk to him, he's good company and often has interesting ideas about velocity and time travel. If I could go back in time, I would want to be a cowboy, with a gun and a badge and a horse that was very, very loyal, like Brave. Vandaline is allergic to all fucking living creatures and prefers plastic flamingos to bring a bit of class to the garden.

When my head gets all messy and I don't know what to do, I write down all of my ideas, on small bits of paper. It's everything that I want to do. When I'm a grown up and I have a real job, then I can do everything. Everything that I want to do. When I don't have to… (*Pause*) When I make Vandaline a cup of tea on a morning and take it to her in bed, or on the sofa, or bathroom floor depending upon where she wanted to sleep, I always have to switch the kettle off just before it boils. Just in that last few milliseconds. If I miss it, and I look away and it boils and clicks, it sends my whole day off. I have to wait until the next day to start again, because that day is ruined then and I can't make it right. No one can.

Act I
Scene 4

Interior day. Crocodiles flat. Beau has come around for coffee, it's a Saturday. Beau is laid on the sofa and Crocodile is standing over her holding her hands above her head. She has a look of concentration on her face. There is spiritual music playing.

Beau

Are you sure you know what you are doing?

Crocodile

Yes, I've told you. I'm a qualified Reiki master. Level 3. I have a certificate. Shh. You need to relax

Beau

I would relax but I'm not sure what you are doing? And last time you tried anything like this on me, I ended up in plaster. Anyway, I thought you didn't like touching people or people touching you. Surely this is mental for you?

Crocodile

You don't touch in Reiki. It's all energy, not physical contact.

Beau

Right. Have you started yet?

Crocodile

I'm sending blue light into you. You are very troubled.

Beau

Yes that because you are waving your arms around like a lunatic, I'm not sure if you are going to karate chop me or break into song. I've had enough. Thank you for trying but I can't relax like this. And seriously, all of this paper?

Beau holds up piles and piles of small bits of paper.

Crocodile

I know. The nails in my head are active today.

Beau

I thought you used to do this, when you were little and lived with her and you didn't get to act on anything you wanted to do?

Crocodile

I know. And then I left. But I didn't really. I just couldn't stop. Do you know what I mean? I still write them.

Beau

I think that woman has a lot to answer for. Vandaline by name, Vandal by nature. Is that even a real name?

Crocodile

That's her name. Her dad was a drinker. He went to register her birth, it was supposed to be Valerie, but after 6 pints, it's all the same.

Beau

Jesus. I'm sorry mate,

Crocodile

It is what it is.

Beau

Beau sits up. Crocodile goes over to the Sofa and starts playing with an engineering contraption, clearly absorbed in it.

I wonder if you could do me a favour? It's Pete. He wants to go out to the new Italian in Camden, but I just can't face a whole evening on my own with him at the moment. He's not in a good place at work and he's rubbish company, doesn't talk. I was thinking…

Crocodile

Of dumping him and going out with that girl in Finance who has been flirting with you for months? *(Crocodile carries on playing with the contraption, getting more absorbed)*

Beau

What? Who? No. I was thinking, that what if you came along and I invited Syd?

Crocodile

Mushroom Syd?

Beau

Mushroom? Oh. Yes, Mushroom Syd.

Crocodile

Will there be Gluten and Dairy Free pasta? But not that hard shit that tastes like garden canes? And will there be harsh overhead lights and music that's too loud and repeats after 88 minutes and toilets that require a special code sequence to flush and hand dryers that make my teeth bend? And waiters that touch your shoulder and breathe. *(Pause)* Because…

Beau

Yes I will request garden cane free pasta, a non-breathing

waiter and all of your other neuro sensitive requirements will

be dealt with. I promise.

Crocodile

Ok, I will stay for 87 minutes in case.

Beau

Great, I will book us a table. I think you will like Syd.

Act I
Scene 5

Interior Day. Inside Crocodiles childhood bedroom. (Recorded and projected above the stage).

Crocodile aged 8

I went to the library today to get some books. I like reading. I have read most of the books in the children's section now. Apart from any about Aliens, because I can't picture Aliens. I don't think they are real and if they are I don't know what they look like and they probably haven't got many fingers. I don't want to start reading the grown up books yet because the book covers often look angry and have sharp and spikey writing which just makes me want to take scissors and trim at them until they sound less like indigestion.

The librarian was very kind to me when I explained this and she has let me borrow AB. Which is every word that begins with A and B all in one book together, called an Encyclopaedia. I am going to learn everything in the world that begins with every letter and start with A. This will help me to sleep, if I can try to remember them all and say them out loud. I will have to do it quietly in case Vandaline comes in. That would not be good. She won't want to hear every word that begins with a fucking A and might even throw the bloody stupid cocking book out of the window, with me after it.

Act I
Scene 6

Interior night. Italian restaurant, small, intimate. Beau and Pete are sitting opposite each other at the table, Crocodile is next to Beau. They are chatting and waiting for Syd to arrive. Syd walks in. Syd is Asian, female, curvy, confident, shoulder length hair, jeans and a jacket, big boots.

Beau

Syd!

Beau and Syd hug, shakes hands with Pete.

Beau

Crocodile, this is Syd.

Crocodile stands up awkwardly. Syd goes to hug her and Crocodile manages to duck it and turn it in to a convoluted hand shake.

Syd

Hi, I'm Syd. Obviously. (*Pauses*) Great to meet you.

Crocodile

Hi. Crocodile.

Syd

Wow, that's an unusual name. Do you have any other names?

Crocodile

Armitage

Syd

I mean like, is it your real name?

Crocodile

What do you mean real name?

Syd

Like, were you born with that name?

Crocodile

No, when I was born I had no name. Vandaline gave me that name. "Skinny little fucking Crocodile" she used to call me. (*Pause*). I shortened it.

Beau

Drinks! Let's order drinks. Pete Beer? Syd? What are you thinking, split a bottle of wine?

Syd

I'd prefer a beer really, something light.

Beau

Sure, Crocodile, what are you in the mood for?

Crocodile

Ginger Beer, no ice. I don't want one of those bottles of Ginger

Beer if the glass that they give me isn't large enough to fit all

of it in at once. And not a warm glass.

Syd

Don't you drink Crocodile?

Crocodile

Yes. (Pause) Just not alcohol.

Act I
Scene 7

Interior Day. Inside Crocodiles childhood bedroom. (Recorded and projected above the stage).

Crocodile

Vandaline is home. She's had her money through and she always likes to sleep it off. (*Pause*) When she gets her money she brings home 3 bottles of Vodka and a chicken to roast. She puts the chicken in the oven and opens a bottle. She sometimes talks about when she was younger and how she wanted to travel and see the world until some little prick got her fucking pregnant and all of her life was over. And she couldn't get rid of the little fucker because it was too late when she realised and he had already fucked off. So here she was in her grandmas cottage raising a weird little fucking brat on her own. (*Pause*) I like chicken day because usually she falls asleep, so I turn off the oven and eat the chicken legs when they are still hot and sticky. It's the only smell in the world that makes me feel solid.

Act I
Scene 8

Interior night. Italian restaurant. They have just finished eating.

Beau

That was amazing. I'm stuffed. We will have to come here

again. I'm very impressed. Syd, what did you think, clean

plate. Can't have been too bad?

Syd

Yeah, really cool thanks. Appreciate you inviting me along. So

how about you Crocodile? We have all swapped our childhood

dreams, what did you want to be?

Crocodile

Since leaving home in Yorkshire, I have always done exactly

what has occurred to me. Because I can. (*Pause*) So every

time that I think that I want to do something, I write it down on

a piece of paper and then I do it.

Syd

Wow, is that possible? Surely you can't just do everything?

That's amazing.

Crocodile

Why not? Everyone always says that it will damage my CV.
Whenever I have a job interview the person hiring always
thinks that they are special enough to be the one to make me
stay. But I don't.

Syd

Haha. That's so cool, I love how your mind works. So what did
you do at University?

Beau

You two should just adopt a cat together now. (*Pause,
exhales*) She smoked too much, slept at the wrong ends of the
day, lived in, what was it 23 houses? And got a 2:1 standing
on her head. Cow.

Crocodile

Criminology with Physics.

Syd

That's a fascinating mix, what made you choose that?

Crocodile

I had just broken up with a bloke that I was seeing, he was eating a boiled egg in bed and it annoyed me. I chose subjects that I thought might hold my concentration for 3 years.

Beau

And what did she do on her first day at University? She went to the library, looked at the past 5 years of exam papers. Worked out the recurring exam questions, mapped that to her seminars and lectures. Attended 4 hours a week and got a fucking 2:1. Whilst muggings here sat in the library day after day doing actual work and scraped through.

Crocodile

It's where you met Pete. Process and efficiency. I don't like over processing anything. What's the point in getting a first? My life would be no different with a first in my honours degree. Just do good enough. Don't get attached. Keep moving.

Beau

She also had about 7 jobs, wrote half a screenplay and set up a Ltd company at the same time. So I'm not quite sure where the efficiency comes in.

Crocodile

It's what occurs to me. I know that may not sound very attractive to most people.

Syd

I think you are very attractive, like – it's attractive. Don't you get tired? This sounds exhausting, but kind of compelling at the same time.

Crocodile

I get tired when I'm bored and doing things that I don't like. It makes me feel panic. So I have to change.

Beau

At work, every few months she swaps desk with someone, for a change of scene. She doesn't ask them like, they just turn up one morning and their stuff has moved, normally to the floor, and she's sitting in their desk with her headphones on.

Syd

Wicked. And you just do that? Don't you mind what people think?

Crocodile

What people think? What do you mean?

Syd

Well, doesn't it upset people? If you just move their stuff?

Crocodile

Oh. Why? It's just a desk. They can move.

Room goes quiet. Awkward silence. Syd is beaming at

Crocodile. Crocodile is oblivious.

Beau

So thanks everyone, it's been a lovely evening. We must do it

again sometime?

Crocodile

Great, cheers. Bank transfer you Beau. (Crocodile stands up)

Pete (nods at Pete). Syd (shakes hand). Good night.

Crocodile leaves the restaurant. Fade to black.

Act I
Scene 9

Interior Day. Inside Crocodiles childhood bedroom. (Recorded and projected above the stage).

Crocodile

Today at school, I threw up on the steps of the main building. I had eaten salt and vinegar crisps on the way to school as we didn't have any bread. Everyone laughed. I had sick on my face. My teacher took me inside, wiped my face and asked me 'Shall I call your mum?' I didn't know what to say. Vandaline was gone, she had been out for days. She would usually come home with some tale about bingo and that fat bastard from the Co-op. I told the teacher about the crisps, that seemed to make everything go away. I was given a glass of water and told to sit in the corridor outside the staff room. It was warm and smelt unenthusiastic. My tummy hurt. I've often wondered how me and my tummy were going to get along long term, as my brain seemed to make it itch and irritate. At least I was avoiding the playground.

Act I
Scene 10

Cut to - Interior Day. Office. Crocodile is sat at her desk with ear phones in, working. Beau walks into the office.

Beau

Croc? Do you have a minute? I'm afraid that I have some bad news my love.

Crocodile takes her headphones off and spins the chair towards Beau.

Crocodile

Yes. I have just ordered a thermal imaging attachment for my phone. Apparently, you can spot pipes leaking and electrical plugs and wires over heating with them.

Beau

Ok darling. But I have some really bad news. Shall we go and find a room?

Crocodile

No, just say it. Talk.

Beau

We had a phone call at the office, because you gave this

number as your emergency contact, as you don't have a land

line and won't listen to voice mails on your mobile.

Crocodile looks impassively at Beau.

Beau

It's your mum darling. I'm afraid that she's passed away.

Crocodile

Passed away? Does that mean died? Why don't people just

day died? Has Vandaline died?

Beau

Yes darling. She was found by a neighbour. They rang an

ambulance, but it was too late. I think she'd been gone a

while.

Crocodile

I wonder what day it was? I always imagined she would die on

a Sunday morning.

Beau

Darling, I don't know. Are you ok? Can I get you anything?

Can I take you home?

Beau hovers around her knowing not to touch her but wanting to give her a hug.

Crocodile

No it's fine. I need to get my other earphones from my coat.

Crocodile leaves the office.

End of Act I.

Act II
Scene 1

Interior day, Crocodiles flat.

Crocodile is seen in her PJs sitting on a sofa watching a pendulum swing back and forth. She restarts it but doesn't otherwise move. There is a large Kayak resting against the wall with an oar.

Knock on the door

Syd

Crocodile? (Pause) Crocodile? (Pause) Are you there?

(Pause) Its' Syd.

Silence. Crocodile lets the pendulum stop swinging.

Knock on the door.

Crocodile stands up slowly and opens the door.

Syd

Hi. Are you ok? I was worried about you. I hope you don't mind. Beau gave me your address. I sent you a few text messages. I know you've had a hard time and I…

Crocodile sits back down on the sofa. Syd hovers for a bit and decides to sit down too but leaves a big enough gap. There is silence for a minute. Syd shuffles.

Crocodile

I was thinking about going for a walk, but the sky looks like its yawning and I don't think that will help.

Syd

I think you're right. (*Pause, shuffles a bit*). The sky doesn't seem in a very good mood today. (*Stands up and walks to bookcase*). When I don't know what to do (*turns hesitantly to Crocodile to see if she is listening*) I take my scrabble board and turn all the letters over so that I can see them and start writing word chains on the board.

Crocodile

It sounds like cheating to me

Syd

Yes, in a way it is. I'm not very good at following rules. But I do like words and patterns and how they interconnect.

Crocodile

Do you ever wonder why oats taste like they have milk in them, when you only add water for porridge? And when you add milk, it doesn't taste any better than water?

Syd

(*Laughing*) Yes! Why would anyone ever add milk?

Silence

Crocodile

No one came.

Syd

Sorry?

Crocodile

Not even the fat bastard from the Co-op.

Syd

(Sitting down) To the funeral (spoken quietly).

Crocodile

They said she had been dead for 3 days before anyone noticed. She fell down the stairs. Tripped on her dressing gown. Drunk. Banged her head. She didn't usually wear a dressing gown. She said they made people look old. She never wanted to be old.

Syd

I'm so sorry

Crocodile

She got her wish. Never being old. She wouldn't have been happy dying in a dressing gown though. Not beige.

Syd

For you I mean. She's your mum.

Crocodile

I'm not sure she was. I need to clear the house. Decide what to do with it and the stuff. For what it's worth.

Syd

Would you like me to come up with you and help? I work for myself, I can easily take some time off.

Crocodile

(*Puts her head up*) Why? You don't even know me. Why would you do that?

Syd

Because I feel like I do. I'd like to help. You've had a bad time and I know how that feels. I just want to help.

Crocodile

Do you have a car?

Syd

Well, a van. I'm a decorator. It's a bit dirty.

Crocodile

Ok let's go.

Syd

When? Now?

Crocodile

Yes of course.

Crocodile gets up and fetches her coat and rucksack and walks to the door. Syd looks a bit startled but follows her out the flat.

Act II

Scene 2

Interior Evening. Crocodiles bedroom in Yorkshire.

Syd and Crocodile are standing in the bedroom, there are cardboard boxes piled everywhere and suitcases.

Syd

Are you sure you want to sell it? You don't think you might want to come back and stay up here sometimes, get out of London?

Crocodile

No, I think I've spent enough time in this room. I want it gone. I could never do anything when I was here. Nothing was ever right.

Syd

What's this? (*Picks up Tupperware box*)

Crocodile

That's Brave.

Syd

Brave?

Crocodile

He's a radish

Syd

Well he might have been. Cool pencil sharpenings.

Crocodile sits down on the bed. She's gone quiet. She lowers her head. She starts to cry quietly. Slow silent sobs. Syd doesn't know what to do, she knows that no one should touch her. She's torn.

Syd

You know, I used to have a pet rat. He attacked and ate the neighbours cat, spat out the bones afterwards. Was a right mess. She was fuming.

Crocodile

Really?

Syd

No, I just made it up.

Crocodile

Why?

Syd

Because it just occurred to me

They both laugh softly. Crocodile wipes her eyes.

Crocodile

I feel tired.

Syd

Shall we clear the bed, do you want to go to sleep?

Crocodile

It's not that kind of tired. My skull feels tired. Like it's been used by someone else, in the wrong way and now I have it back, its annoyed and doesn't want to be a skull anymore.

Syd

I see. (*Pauses*) What do you think your skull needs to feel better?

Crocodile

Its needs a defrag. You know like on old pc's where you had to run a defragmentation programme to get the contents of the hard drive back in order again. I used to like doing that and watching the graphic change, the before and after picture.

Syd

Yes my mum used to do that to her laptop. I know exactly what you mean. Is there anything that you used to do as a kid that would help when you needed to calm down?

Crocodile

I used to count things. When my brain got too busy and came

up with hundreds of ideas that I needed to act on… I would try

to stop them by counting…

Syd
Ok, what like?
Crocodile
Like this (points to the bed), this (points to the chair), this

(door), this (desk), this (book case) and this (Mirror). 6 things.

And I would lay on my bed and imagine the 6 things in my

mind and as I counted them I would tense my muscles up. So

1 bed, left bicep, 2 chair, right bicep, 3 door left thigh, 4 desk,

right thigh, 5 bookcase left bicep, 6 mirror right bicep. Then

repeat, for as long as I needed to.

Syd

Do you want to try?

Crocodile

You don't think I'm weird?

Syd

Not at all, come on let's try.

They clear the bed and lay on it. One at either end.

Both together

1 bed, left bicep, (*Syd hesitates and catches up*) 2 chair, right bicep, 3 door left thigh, 4 desk, right thigh, 5 bookcase left bicep (*Syd slightly behind again*), 6 mirror right bicep

Syd

Again

. Both together

1 bed, 2 chair, 3 door, 4 desk, 5 bookcase, 6 mirror. 1 bed, 2 chair, 3 door, 4 desk, 5 bookcase, 6 mirror. 1 bed, 2 chair, 3 door, 4 desk, 5 bookcase, 6 mirror.

Syd

This is great. It's like a meditation or a chant. I can totally see why you do this. And adding the muscle thing, means that the body starts to relax too. Its genius.

. Both together

1 bed, 2 chair, 3 door, 4 desk, 5 bookcase, 6 mirror. 1 bed, 2 chair, 3 door, 4 desk, 5 bookcase, 6 mirror.

Syd

Thank you for showing me this and for letting me into your world. I want to understand you.

Crocodile

Thank you. Most people can just sense that I'm weird and stay away from me or be mean. Why aren't you mean?

Syd

I would never be mean to you. I think your mind is amazing. Your drive and energy and certainty. I wish I had 10% of it and I wouldn't be a single, penniless decorator who eats a tub of Ben and Jerrys every week after slimming group all on my own.

Crocodile

Why do you need to go to slimming group?

Syd

Ha, thanks! I need to shed a few pounds. It helps me stay focused and eating healthily. I could cook for you if you would like? Just natural ingredients, nothing dodgy. You are gluten and dairy free aren't you?

Crocodile

Yes and I don't like cooked peas.

Syd

Well there you go then. My signature chicken bake in the oven

will be just the job. Let me know and I will rustle it up for you.

Crocodile

Why are you being so nice to me?

Syd

Because I think you are a good person and you are having a

hard time right now. Because I like you.

Crocodile

I don't dislike you.

They are both very close now, the tension can be felt.

Crocodile stands up decidedly.

Crocodile

Right. We need to go.

Syd

Now? Back to London?

Crocodile

Yes. Come on. I've emailed the estate agent and its going on the market tomorrow morning. I have what I need in boxes and a clearance company is coming on Tuesday for the rest of the things. I need to move on.

Syd

Like right now?

Crocodile

Yes. Come on.

Crocodile leaves the room.

Act II
Scene 3

Interior Day. Crocodiles Flat. Syd is at the house. She is sitting on the sofa. Syd is measuring something in a conical flask.

Syd

It's a shame you didn't come around last night. The dinner I made you was really lovely. I think you would have liked it.

Crocodile

Maybe. (Carries on measuring)

Syd

It might have been good to get a text or something, saying that you couldn't come?

Crocodile

I get that (*adds more ingredients to the flask*)

Syd

I understand that you are busy, but it might be nice if we could just hang out a bit more? Get to know each other maybe?

Nothing heavy.

Crocodile

I see.

Syd

I'm not really looking for anything. I'm just sort of a bit lonely

and looking for someone to do things with sometimes.

Crocodile

Right.

Syd

Do you think maybe you could sit down and we perhaps chat

a little?

Crocodile

(*Becomes alert abruptly*) This isn't going to work.

Syd

What, your experiment or whatever it is?

Crocodile

No, not this. No. I don't know. Maybe.

Syd

What, Me?

Crocodile

Yes you, us. Whatever this is. I haven't got time for it. You are

being too demanding. This isn't what I want. It's totally and

utterly not at all even conceivably close to anything that

resembles something remotely similar to my aspirations.

(*Wanders around clicking her fingers*)

Syd

What? (*Stands up*) Because I made you dinner and you didn't

turn up or text and I'm too demanding?

Crocodile

Yes, sorry. No. Yes. I can't do this right now. It's not working.

You will have to leave. I can't, I just can't. I need my space

and my freedom and I need to be able to do whatever I want,

whatever it is, without anyone telling me that I can or can't or

that it's stupid or impetuous or ill thought through. And there

you are all of the time, in my head. Your smell... in my

thoughts. I just can't... (*Paces and stutters*)

Syd

But I haven't even done anything, or asked you for anything?

Crocodile

It's not that you have or haven't done anything. I can't seem to think any more. All I can think about is you. What you've said, what you've done. What you might think. It's driving me mad. I need to focus on what I am doing, not think about you. (*Pause*) I can't just stop all of the time and have meals.

Syd

So don't, just "be".

Crocodile

(*Walks around very agitatedly and speaks very fast. Seems almost angry*) Don't you see that's exactly the most ridiculous thing that you could say to me and here you are standing right in front of me asking me, Me? A zebra, what the square root of 187 is? It's futile.

Syd

I don't know what to say.

Crocodile

Precisely.

Syd

Wow. Seriously. You are kidding me. Ok. I will leave, but it's

your loss. Wow.

Syd leaves very upset. Door slams. Crocodile flinches and

then carries on with the experiment.

Act II
Scene 4

Interior day. London office. Beau and Crocodile are at the desk, but opposite sides this time.

Beau

So Croc, how are things?

Crocodile

(Carries on working) Fine.

Beau

With Syd?

Crocodile

Fine.

Beau

Are you going to make me do the 5 question thing, where you will evade and avoid me until I get to question 5 and then you will answer?

Crocodile

Most people don't notice that you haven't answered their question. Most people move on at 2 at the latest.

Beau

I'm not most people. Talk to me. Syd is really upset.

Crocodile

She's too much. She wants too much. She makes my brain

not work properly. I can't cope with how needy she is.

Beau

I really don't think that she's needy. She practically brought up

both of her younger brothers on her own, as her mum as was

always out at work. She's really not.

Crocodile

She's just stuck in my head like a screensaver. I can't switch it

off. She asks too many questions. I think I might text James

again and see if he wants to hang out.

Beau

You couldn't stand him in the end. Don't do that. He doesn't

get you at all, or even try to understand you. I don't like the

way he speaks to you when he has had a drink. Doesn't

sound to me like you don't like her... maybe you protest too

much?

Crocodile

He's not that bad. I kind of liked him. (*Pause*) No, I'm not

protesting.

Beau

He is that bad. He's more interested in Motor Cross than he is

in you. Don't go backwards. I know you are having a bad time.

You need someone who understands you and appreciates

you for who you are, we both know someone like that.

Crocodile

But men are just less complicated. You know where you

stand. There's no emotional drama. They know what they

want. They don't make your head feel like liquidised

pineapple. It's simple. I like it.

Beau

It's your life. But I think it's a mistake. That girl is really into

you and you've treated her pretty badly.

Act II
Scene 5

Interior day, Crocodiles flat. She is in bed. Full of cold. Coughing and sneezing. She starts to get out of bed for a drink. Feels too bad and gives up. Gets back in bed. Lights dim to show its now night time.

Act II
Scene 6

Interior night, Crocodiles flat. She is in bed. Full of cold. Clearly hasn't been out of bed. She manages to get up. Gets the kettle off the side and the door knocks. Crocodile slowly walks to the door carrying the kettle. Sneezing and coughing. She opens the door.

Syd

Hi (*She is carrying lemons, honey and a bag of medicines*). I caught up with Beau. I heard you had the flu and I was passing.

Syd takes the kettle off Crocodile and walks her back over to the bed. Crocodile gets in bed. Syd makes the drink and takes it over to her. Then goes to lie down on the sofa and pulls a blanket over herself.

Act II
Scene 7

Interior day, Crocodiles flat. She is in bed. Syd is still on the sofa.

Crocodile

Syd?

Syd

(*Sitting up slowly*) Yes Croc

Crocodile

Did you bring your scrabble board with you?

Syd

(*Laughing*) Feeling a bit better then are we?

Crocodile

Maybe. (Pause) I don't want to go to work today. I can't face it. I can't face Git Boy. I can't write one more paper on contrived nonsense. I actually can't bring myself to. It makes me feel compromised.

Syd

(*Getting off the sofa and sitting next to Crocodile on the bed*)

You don't have to do anything that you don't want to do. I'm here for you, you know. You can try and push me away, but I'm stubborn. I know we have a connection. I know you feel it too. I will keep coming back.

Crocodile

Maybe I needed to know that. Maybe I needed to know that you wouldn't leave, even when pushed. I find it hard…

Syd

Go on

Crocodile

I can't talk when it's light. Can you draw the curtains a bit more? I can't talk if you can see me. It has to be dark or you have to be away.

Syd gets up and draws the curtains and turns the lamp down.

Crocodile

Thank you. (*Pause*). I could never "be" with Vandaline. In her presence I would try to be as normal as possible. I would try to think about how someone else could be, in my place, how would they act. To escape the confusion. I watch people to learn how to respond. How to jump into conversations, to not cut people off when they are speaking. To feign interest when they are boring me to distraction. It's so hard. (Pause). I would think of characters from novels who I liked. Heathcliffe. What would he do? How would he cope with her? He grew up wild and gnashed and gnarled and spoke his mind. He and Vandaline would not have got on either. (*Pauses*). Maybe if I could have been charming like the Great Gatsby, but he was faking it too and would probably have got her even more drunk. (*Pause*).

I couldn't imagine being a woman. That was always so difficult for me. I was always male. Sherlock Holmes sometimes. Vandaline didn't care much for women anyway. She never had any female friends. They were always men that she had over.

Syd

Can I ask you about your dad? Do you know?

Crocodile

No. I have no idea. She never said. He just was. (*Pause*). I often wonder. If I'm like him. I wonder if (pause), it's where I get my (*pause*) difference from. Being autistic.

Syd

Really, do you think? Have you been told that you are autistic?

Crocodile

Yes, 18 months ago. We did some psychology and aptitude tests at work, as part of some research thing with the University and my results came out different. They asked me if I minded doing more tests, I said no. I didn't care. Whatever. They told me I was autistic and had ADHD.

Syd

And how did that make you feel?

Crocodile

Feel is a funny word for me. I understand think. But I find feel quite difficult. I know what anger is and bored and intrigued. I've been sad, I know that. But I'm not sure about other feelings.

Syd

What about Love? Dare I ask, do you mind? Have you ever been in love?

Crocodile

Maybe. I'm not sure. I tend to just spend time with people that I'm attracted to and then when I'm not. I leave them.

Syd

Has anyone every left you? Broken your heart?

Crocodile

I guess I don't give them the chance. My longest relationship was with Matt for 7 months and that was only because we were working on our dissertations together and he would reserve me a computer in the library. My shortest was with Alex, she only lasted a weekend. That was enough. She was a model or something.

Syd

You are so lovely. I love the way that you think. How the world

looks from your eyes. I just want to hear more and understand

you.

Crocodile

I wish I could understand me too. Thanks for listening and

giving a damn.

Syd

Always.

Crocodile

Do you want some soup? I want tomato soup.

Act II
Scene 8

Interior Night. London office, Beau and Syd are the last in the office.

Beau

We could have met at the pub you know

Syd

I know, I was just…

Beau

Hoping to bump into Croc….?

Syd

Busted!

Beau

Ha! She's in the other office this afternoon, you missed her. Hey, I'm glad that she's started opening up to you. She doesn't do that. Not easily. You must have made a connection.

Syd

Yes, it's been brilliant, seeing her unfold. I'm fascinated. And I just think she's totally gorgeous, kind of sexy quirky, just love her energy.

Beau

Yes she's ace, Croc is one of a kind. But she's very off at the moment. With her mother dying and actually… since her diagnosis. She took that so fucking hard. A bloke that she was seeing at the time, said that she became "more autistic", that her behaviours were more exaggerated, since she got the formal result. The stupid fuck dumped Croc, said that he "hadn't signed up for this shit".

Syd

Wow, seriously? That's brutal.

Beau

Croc said to him, imagine you were a straight man for your whole life and then at 40 you finally decide that you are no longer going to live a lie and you come out of the closet as gay. A seemingly straight man, now wearing a pink feather bower and leather pants prancing around town, because he can.

Syd

There is more than a little irony here

Beau

I know. That's how she tells it.. Like she has a feather boa. She told me last week that she's been holding her breath, copying, watching, and trying to work out how to be "neurotypical" her whole life and now she's not prepared to pretend any more. So probably, yes she is a camp man.

Syd

There are so many stereotypes around this stuff, I googled it and it's still hard to understand exactly what it is because everyone is different.

Beau

People expect Rain Man. Crocs not like that. None of my mates on the spectrum are, you can't generalise that much. Women autistics are different to men as well, you just can't lump people together – it's like anything.

Syd

Yes that makes sense; I mean generally women kind of mask their behaviours better as they are expected to moderate their behaviour, even neurotypical. I know I do – a lot. Do you know if the list writing thing is part of her Autism?

Beau

Yes, partly and also because of her - Vandaline her mother. She says she feels like there is a lion chasing her if she doesn't keep moving, if she doesn't keep writing her plans down, it will catch her up. I've been trying to help her for years. It needs to click in her head first before I think any of us can help. I just try to be there for her and take the piss out of her to keep her you know, grounded.

Syd

You do, I've heard you – you are harsh! Harsh woman!

Beau

Croc and I are cool. She will get through this. She just needs to deal with this grief and finally let that evil woman go.

Syd

Totally agree with that. At least my mum was just absent, didn't inflict any direct damage, just bloody worked all of the time. Mothers. Anyway… I have an idea that I want to try out with Croc…

Beau

I don't think I want to know…. Come on – pub.

Interior day. Crocodiles bedroom in the cottage.

Piles of small pieces of paper next to the bed. (Recorded and

projected above the stage).

Crocodile

Vandaline was crying last night. I don't quite know why but I

could hear her in her bedroom through the wall. I ran down the

stairs and got a box of Frosties and brought them up. I put my

trunk behind the door. It's never a good sign when she's

crying. You never know which way it will go. Sometimes she

drinks and that cheers her up so that she starts singing and

reminiscing. Often she gets angry and uses lots of words that

don't mean anything and they sound like gravy being poured

onto a record player. It's best to eat cereal and read my

books. I'm on M now. I'm not a big fan of M, I don't like the

way that the letter looks. How it could be a W trying to trick

you, or an N that got dragged on too long. I don't know if she

has gone out now, or if she is still in there. I didn't hear the

front door go and I waited to hear all night. I'm just going to sit

in here for a while longer, just until she settles.

Act II
Scene 10

Interior day. Crocodiles flat in London

Crocodile has a drill and is drilling the wall. She has goggles on and an over the top bandana.

Crocodile

There. Where's the stupid board to put up?

Syd

What Crocodile actually said was, (aping Crocodile) thank you darling for this very thoughtful pinboard that I am going to write all of my good ideas on. And if they are still on there in a months time then I am allowed to consider them. But until then I'm not allowed to do ANYTHING.

Crocodile

A whole month? I'm not allowed to do anything at all?

Syd

Nope, you have to write it on a piece of paper and stick it on the board and leave it.

Crocodile

A whole month. You know that's like 3,000 years in my brain.

That's all I know how to do – just act, on anything. It keeps me

moving, it keeps me out of that house in Yorkshire.

Syd

That's the point. Leave it to settle. If you write it down, instead

of doing it. You might be able to let all of that go? Leave it in

the past and let yourself move on. Let Vandaline go.

Crocodile

Not doing things? Are you meant to be good for me? My

Crazy woman. (*Crocodile leans in closer but does not touch*

her)

Syd

Crocodile, if only you knew it.

Act II
Scene 11

Interior Day, Office

Beau and Crocodile are sat at their desks. They are back in

the original positions.

Beau

Am I buying a hat yet?

Crocodile?

If you want to. Why are you asking me? Buy three.

Beau

It means, are you and Syd getting it on?

Crocodile

Getting on what?

Beau

Together. You know exactly what I'm talking about. Don't go

all literal on me just because it suits.

Crocodile

We are friends. She's helping me out with my lists and not

doing things.

Beau

Friends, sure thing. And how is the list going?

Crocodile

I've got 367 things on the pin board at the moment and 5 days

to go. I have only lapsed and done 3 things.

Beau

Oh god. What are they? You imported a gibbon from a

sanctuary in Malawi?

Crocodile

No. I bought a new suit. Got a new job and quit this one.

Beau

What? When were you going to tell me that?

Crocodile

I just did.

Act II
Scene 12

Interior Night. Crocodiles flat in London

Crocodile

I heard a little girl on the tube telling her mother, that it's not at all easy to turn yourself into a waffle cone. I kind of know what she means.

Syd

Absolutely. I can see that being challenging.

Crocodile

I need to buy some more drawing pins. I have none. But I didn't know if that counted as me being spontaneous and doing things, so I wrote it on a piece of paper and used a peeling knife to stick it to the board.

Syd

(Laughing) Don't worry, I will pick you some up. How does it feel not "doing" all of the time?

Crocodile

It felt like I had cling film over my hands to start with. But now I'm quite enjoying it. I think because I have the act of writing it down and pinning it up, it doesn't quite feel like I'm doing nothing. It really helps. Thank you. Thank you for everything that you have done.

Syd

You did all the hard work

Crocodile

You know what I mean. I'm saying thank you. It means a lot. You've stuck around and don't call me names or wince when I say things to people that inadvertently make them cry.

Syd

It a pleasure. I just want to help. I'm so glad that it's working and that you are finally setting. Not constantly fiddling and trying to achieve something. It's nice to see you breathe.

Crocodile

Thank you. Really. For the first time in my life I feel still. Not racing to achieve something. Not trying to be something.

Syd

That's amazing. I'm so pleased for you. Really I am. (*Pause*)

Did you want anything else to eat?

Crocodile

Yes. But sit there. I have something for you.

Crocodile goes to the freezer and gets out a pot. She passes it to Syd with two spoons.

Syd

Ha! Ben and Jerrys. My favourite. Thank you.

Crocodile

And you are not eating it alone.

Syd

But you don't like dairy or cold things or sharing food?

Crocodile

But I feel like breaking rules tonight.

They kiss.

End of Act II

Exterior Dusk. On a beach, sat around a small campfire, Beau, Syd and Crocodile. They have blankets. No one is talking. They are watching the fire.

Syd

What is it about watching fire that is so compelling? I could watch it for hours. That and aquariums. I never tire of watching the fish. Hours…

Beau

Well I'm freezing my knackers off here. Crocodile. Have you brought the pot?

Crocodile

Reaches behind her and brings out the cooking pot from the opening scene.

Yes

Beau

And have you got the lists and little bits of paper?

Crocodile

Reaches behind her and brings out a large pile of shredded paper.

Yes

Beau

And is it absolutely everything? You wrote down every single half assed idea that you had?

Crocodile

It's the full list of every single thing that has occurred to me for the last month and I haven't acted on any of them. I have written them up and stuck them to the pin board. Sometimes I rearranged them and had to add further detail, when extra ideas came into my head. It's a full catalogue.

Beau

And is Amazon now out of business?

Crocodile

No. I believe they have survived the month without me. (Pause) That was a joke, Hey? Beau, we did a joke together.

Beau

We did a joke Crocodile.

Syd

I'm really proud of you baby. (*She looks at Beau*). We both

are.

Crocodile

It's over you know.

Syd

I know baby.

Crocodile

I don't feel as wired anymore. (*Pause*) Sometimes, when I was

thinking something, before, (*pause*) maybe about Chinese

fabric and there's a song on in my head, whilst I'm counting or

trying to sort through something else and then someone

speaks to me. It felt like a physical assault. Like I can't cope

with their words at the same time as all of my brain and I don't

know how to tell them that, so I walk off or shout something to

try to get over the noise. But it's getting easier, I have less

tracks on at once.

Beau

That's great babe. Like a reduced Spotify subscription.

Crocodile

Yes. Exactly that. You know, last year I listened to the same

song for 26 hours. I did have a break, you know, I'm not crazy.

I just had it on repeat for days. And if I didn't pay close

attention to the words, I had to start the song again and give it

proper attention.

Syd

You are doing brilliant baby, managing the noise and stress.

Really brilliant.

Crocodile

I know that I don't need to panic now. I know that I'm not

trapped in a little room and that I can do things in my own

time. Without worrying about her and what she might do next.

A constant presence. (*Pause*) Not drinking coffee helps. The

caffeine. Or 22 cups of Green Tea. That helps.

Beau

And never Red Bull babe, never the hard stuff.

They all sit quietly watching the fire

Crocodile

I wanted to tell you something. (*Pauses*) I wanted to tell you

(*Pauses*). My name (*Pauses*)

Syd takes Crocodiles hand.

(*Pauses*)

It's Annabel.

Crocodile lets go of Syds hand and sets the paper alight in the

cooking pot and it burns slowly. They sit and watch for a few

minutes.

Goodbye Vandaline.

Curtain falls.

The End

Printed in Great Britain
by Amazon